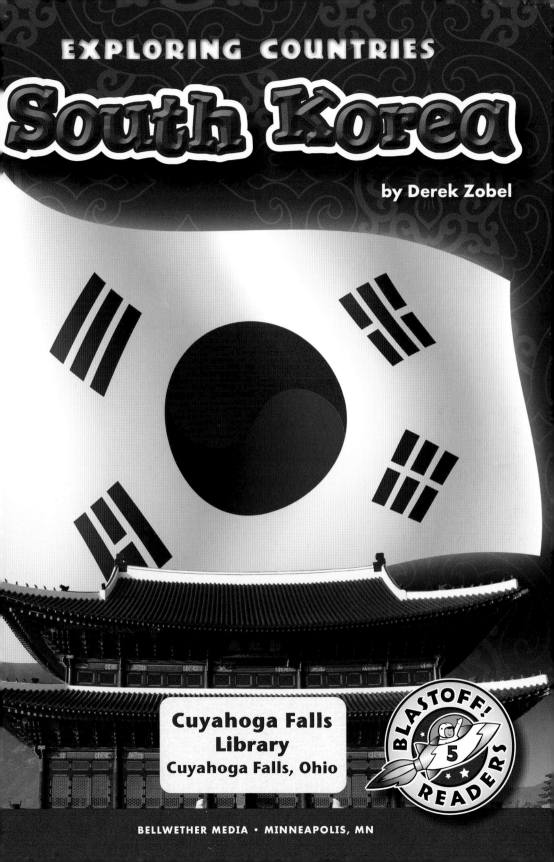

EXPLORING COUNTRIES

South Korea

by Derek Zobel

BLASTOFF! READERS
5

BELLWETHER MEDIA • MINNEAPOLIS, MN

Note to Librarians, Teachers, and Parents:

Blastoff! Readers are carefully developed by literacy experts and combine standards-based content with developmentally appropriate text.

Level 1 provides the most support through repetition of high-frequency words, light text, predictable sentence patterns, and strong visual support.

Level 2 offers early readers a bit more challenge through varied simple sentences, increased text load, and less repetition of high-frequency words.

Level 3 advances early-fluent readers toward fluency through increased text and concept load, less reliance on visuals, longer sentences, and more literary language.

Level 4 builds reading stamina by providing more text per page, increased use of punctuation, greater variation in sentence patterns, and increasingly challenging vocabulary.

Level 5 encourages children to move from "learning to read" to "reading to learn" by providing even more text, varied writing styles, and less familiar topics.

Whichever book is right for your reader, Blastoff! Readers are the perfect books to build confidence and encourage a love of reading that will last a lifetime!

This edition first published in 2012 by Bellwether Media, Inc.

No part of this publication may be reproduced in whole or in part without written permission of the publisher. For information regarding permission, write to Bellwether Media, Inc., Attention: Permissions Department, 5357 Penn Avenue South, Minneapolis, MN 55419.

Library of Congress Cataloging-in-Publication Data
Zobel, Derek, 1983-
South Korea / by Derek Zobel.
    p. cm. – (Exploring countries) (Blastoff! readers)
Summary: "Developed by literacy experts for students in grades three through seven, this book introduces young readers to the geography and culture of South Korea"–Provided by publisher.
Includes bibliographical references and index.
ISBN 978-1-60014-624-4 (hardcover : alk. paper)
1. Korea (South)–Juvenile literature. I. Title.
DS907.4.Z63 2012
951.95–dc22   2011002233

Printed in the United States of America, North Mankato, MN.

080111   1187

Contents

Where Is South Korea?   4

The Land   6

Cheju Island   8

Wildlife   10

The People   12

Daily Life   14

Going to School   16

Working   18

Playing   20

Food   22

Holidays   24

Kyongbok Palace   26

Fast Facts   28

Glossary   30

To Learn More   31

Index   32

Where Is South Korea?

North
Korea

Sea
of
Japan

★ Seoul

South
Korea

Yellow
Sea

N

W · E

S

Korea Strait

Cheju ➡

Did you know?

North Korea and South Korea used to be one country. After World War II, that country split into northern and southern parts.

Japan

South Korea is a country in eastern Asia. It covers 38,502 square miles (99,720 square kilometers). This includes the southern part of the Korean **peninsula** and over 3,000 islands. The northern part of the Korean peninsula belongs to North Korea, the only country that borders South Korea. The Sea of Japan washes onto the eastern shore of South Korea. The Yellow Sea laps against the western coast of the country. To the south, Japan lies across the Korea **Strait**. Cheju, South Korea's largest island, is located in this strait. South Korea's capital, Seoul, is found in the northwestern part of the country.

Mountains cover most of the landscape in South Korea. The two main mountain ranges are the T'aebaek Mountains and the Sobaek Mountains. The T'aebaek range stretches along the eastern coast and up into North Korea. The Sobaek range runs in an S-shape across South Korea. The Han, Kum, and Naktong rivers all start in the T'aebaek Mountains. They flow down into the lowlands and empty into the Yellow Sea or the Korea Strait. Plains, rolling hills, and river basins can be found in the western and southeastern parts of the country.

Sobaek Mountains

fun fact

The Han River flows through Seoul.
It has been a part of Korean history
for thousands of years.

South Korea's Cheju Island rises above the surface of the Korea Strait. The highest mountain in South Korea, Mount Halla, is found on the island. It is an **extinct** volcano that rises to 6,398 feet (1,950 meters). Thousands of years ago, **lava** flowed through **lava tubes** on the island. Today, these tubes are large caves. A **crater** with a lake lies at the top of Mount Halla. This mountain and the surrounding area are a national park. Thousands of people visit this park and the lava tubes every year.

lava tube

long-tailed goral

Mandarin duck

northern pika

fun fact

The northern pika is found throughout South Korea. This rodent has a reddish brown coat in the summer and a grayish brown coat in the winter.

South Korea is home to many different animals. Lynx, brown bears, and several kinds of deer roam the forests that cover the mountain slopes. The **endangered** long-tailed goral also shares this **habitat**. Only about 250 long-tailed gorals remain in South Korea.

Did you know?
Korean water deer are great swimmers. They can swim to islands in rivers and lakes to escape from predators!

Korean water deer

Several animals live in the country's lowlands and rivers. Korean water deer are plentiful in the **wetlands**. They must watch out for black bears that come to the water's edge in search of food. Pheasants, cranes, and Mandarin ducks also live near rivers and lakes throughout the country.

More than 48.5 million people live in South Korea.
Almost all of them have **ancestors** who were
native to the land thousands of years ago.
The country is also home to many Chinese people.
Recently, **immigrants** have come to South Korea
from countries in central Asia to find work.

South Koreans speak Korean, the official language of the country. Many people also speak English, which is now taught in the country's schools. Since South Korea was once ruled by Japan, many older South Koreans still know Japanese.

Speak Korean!

Korean is written in characters. However, Korean words can be written in English so you can read them out loud!

English	Korean	How to say it
hello	an-nyeong-ha-se-yo	ahn-yung-hah-seh-oh
good-bye	an-nyeong-hi ka-se-yo	ahn-yung-hee kah-seh-oh
yes	ye	yeh
no	a-ni-yo	ah-nee-oh
thank you	kam-sa-ham-ni-da	kahm-sah-hahm-nee-dah
please	chom/che-bal	chom/cheh-ball
friend	ch'in-gu	cheen-goo

About four out of every five South Koreans live in cities. They live in large apartment buildings or have houses in the **suburbs**. Many of South Korea's cities have trains and buses that people take around. However, most South Koreans own cars that they drive from place to place. The cities are full of supermarkets, malls, and stores where people buy food and other goods.

In the countryside, people live in small towns or on farms. They mainly use cars to travel around. Most towns have stores and supermarkets where people buy food and goods. Many South Koreans also use the Internet to buy products, which are delivered right to their homes.

Where People Live in South Korea

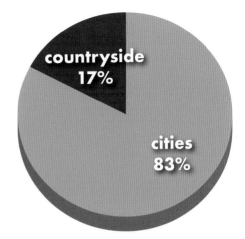

countryside 17%

cities 83%

fun fact

In South Korea, it is a tradition to remove your shoes before you enter someone's house.

South Korean children must go to school for nine years. They attend elementary school for the first six years and middle school for the next three. They study math, science, social studies, Korean, and English at these levels. After middle school, they can choose to attend high school or **vocational school**. Students who go to a vocational school are trained to do specific jobs. Those who complete high school can apply to universities.

Many compete to get into South Korea's top universities.

fun fact

Many classrooms in South Korea are starting to use robots to help children learn.

Where People Work in South Korea

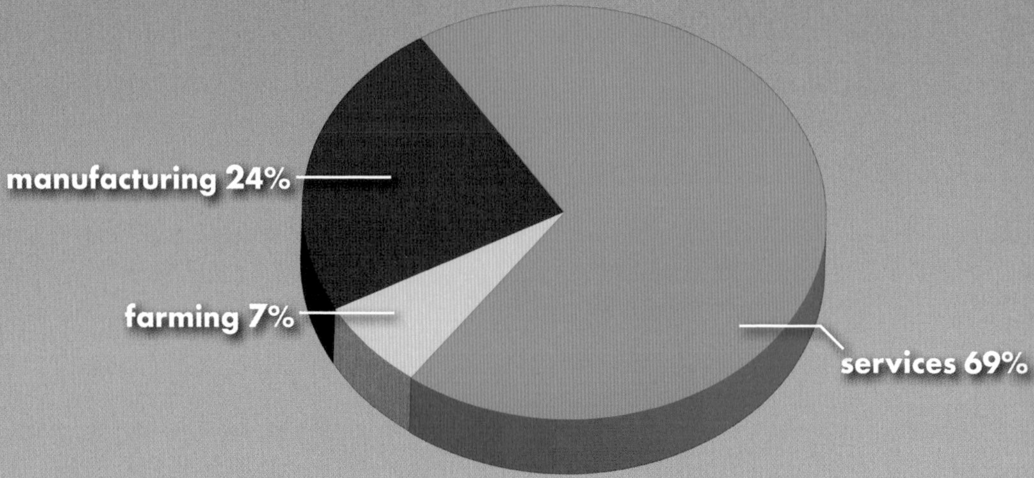

manufacturing 24%

farming 7%

services 69%

Did you know?
South Korea makes more ships than any other country in the world!

Most South Koreans have **service jobs**. They work in banks, schools, police stations, and other places that serve people. Many South Koreans work in factories that make cars, electronics, chemicals, and other products. In the country's **ports**, workers build large ships that are sold to countries around the world.

In the countryside, most people are miners or farmers. Miners dig up **minerals** from the earth and send them to factories in the cities. Farmers grow rice, barley, tea, tangerines, pears, and cabbage. Some raise pigs and cattle. Others use dairy cows to make milk and cheese. Along the coasts, fishermen haul in many kinds of fish and seafood.

ssirum

South Koreans enjoy many sports and activities. The martial art of *tae kwon do* is one of South Korea's national sports. The other national sport is *ssirum*, a style of wrestling where each wrestler tries to push the other out of the ring. South Korea also has baseball and soccer leagues.

Video games are very popular across South Korea. Most people play video games in their homes. In cities, they can pay to play video games inside stores. Some games have their own leagues where people are paid to compete!

fun fact
Video gamers often go head-to-head in front of large crowds in South Korea. Winners can take home thousands of dollars!

Did you know?

Tea is a popular drink in South Korea. People use roots, leaves, grains, and fruits to make many kinds of tea.

South Koreans eat a lot of rice, vegetables, and meat. *Kimchi* is served with almost every meal in the country. To make it, people **pickle** vegetables in a mixture of ginger, garlic, peppers, and other ingredients. It is sometimes cooked in soups and stews.

Bibimbap is a spicy dish South Koreans enjoy. It is a mixture of egg, rice, and vegetables tossed in a hot sauce. Sometimes it contains meat or seafood. Another favorite is *pulgogi*, which is barbecued beef, pork, or chicken cooked over an open fire. Rice cakes, or *tteok*, are popular desserts throughout the country.

bibimbap

kimchi

Children's Day

fun fact

May 5 is Children's Day in South Korea.
On this day, parents take their kids to
the zoo, a museum, or the movies.
Large parades and speeches mark the
holiday throughout the country.

South Korea has many holidays that honor the country's
history. On October 3, National Foundation Day
celebrates the day over 4,000 years ago when the first
Korean state was founded. *Gwangbokjeol*, or Restoration
of Light Day, falls on August 15. It remembers the day
that Korea became free from Japanese rule at the end
of World War II. On July 17, 1948, South Korea signed
its **constitution**. This day is celebrated every year as
Constitution Day.

Christianity and Buddhism are the two main religions in South Korea. Buddhists celebrate Buddha's birthday, which falls in the month of May. Christians celebrate Christmas, Easter, and other Christian holidays.

Did you know?
Celebrations of Buddha's birthday feature large dragons. The dragons stand for positive energy and creativity.

Buddha's birthday

In 1394, King Taejo of Korea built the Kyongbok Palace in Seoul. Many later kings added to the palace. In the 1500s, Japan invaded Seoul and burned many of the palace buildings. Korea rebuilt the palace in the 1800s. It soon included over 300 buildings and more than 5,000 rooms. In the early 1900s, Japan once again invaded and destroyed most of the palace buildings.

Blue House

fun fact

The Kyongbok Palace is next to the Blue House, which is where the President of South Korea lives.

After South Korea gained its independence from Japan, the people wanted to restore Kyongbok Palace. In 1989, the South Korean government started a program to rebuild most of the old palace buildings. Today, the palace stands as a symbol of South Korea's history and independence.

Fast Facts About South Korea

South Korea's Flag

The flag of South Korea has a red and blue circle in the middle. The circle is surrounded by four sets of black bars that stand for the sun, moon, earth, and heaven. The circle in the middle stands for the origin and balance of the universe. The white background stands for peace. The flag was first adopted in 1948. It has had minor changes since then.

Official Name: Republic of Korea

Area: 38,502 square miles
(99,720 square kilometers);
South Korea is the 108th largest
country in the world.

Capital City:	Seoul
Important Cities:	Busan, Incheon, Daegu
Population:	48,754,657 (July 2011)
Official Language:	Korean
National Holiday:	Restoration of Light Day (August 15)
Religions:	None (49.3%), Christian (26.3%), Buddhist (23.2%), Other (1.2%)
Major Industries:	farming, fishing, manufacturing, services, shipbuilding
Natural Resources:	coal, graphite, lead, tungsten
Manufactured Products:	electronics, cars, chemicals, steel, ships
Farm Products:	rice, barley, tea, citrus fruits, pears, cabbage, ginseng, cattle, pigs, chickens, dairy products
Unit of Money:	South Korean won

Glossary

ancestors—relatives who lived long ago

constitution—the basic principles and laws of a nation

crater—a large, bowl-shaped hole in the earth

endangered—close to becoming extinct

extinct—no longer active; extinct volcanoes can never become active again.

habitat—the environment in which a plant or animal usually lives

immigrants—people who leave one country to live in another country

lava—hot, melted rock that flows from volcanoes

lava tubes—tunnels made from cooled lava that hardens around hotter, flowing lava

minerals—elements found in nature; lead and tungsten are examples of minerals.

native—originally from a specific place

peninsula—a section of land that extends out from a larger piece of land and is almost completely surrounded by water

pickle—to preserve in a mixture for use at a later date; South Koreans often pickle vegetables to make *kimchi*.

ports—sea harbors where ships can dock; ships from around the world deliver and pick up goods in South Korea's ports.

service jobs—jobs that perform tasks for people or businesses

strait—a narrow stretch of water that connects two larger bodies of water

suburbs—communities that lie just outside a city

vocational school—a school that trains students to do specific jobs

wetlands—wet, spongy lands; bogs, marshes, and swamps are wetlands.

To Learn More

AT THE LIBRARY

Jackson, Tom. *South Korea*. Washington, D.C.: National Geographic, 2007.

Miller, Jennifer A. *South Korea*. Minneapolis, Minn.: Lerner, 2010.

Walters, Tara. *South Korea*. New York, N.Y.: Children's Press, 2008.

ON THE WEB

Learning more about South Korea is as easy as 1, 2, 3.

1. Go to www.factsurfer.com.

2. Enter "South Korea" into the search box.

3. Click the "Surf" button and you will see a list of related Web sites.

With factsurfer.com, finding more information is just a click away.

Index

activities, 20, 21
Blue House, 27
Buddha's birthday, 25
capital (see Seoul)
Cheju Island, 4, 5, 8-9
Children's Day, 24
Constitution Day, 24
daily life, 14-15
education, 16-17
food, 22-23
Gwangbokjeol (Restoration of
  Light Day), 24
Han River, 6, 7
holidays, 24-25
housing, 14-15
King Taejo, 26
Korea Strait, 4, 5, 6, 9
Korean peninsula, 5
Kyongbok Palace, 26-27
landscape, 6-9
languages, 13
location, 4-5
Mount Halla, 9
national park, 9
peoples, 12
Seoul, 4, 5, 7, 26
Sobaek Mountains, 6, 7
sports, 20
transportation, 14-15

wildlife, 10-11
working, 18-19